# Ultra-Violet

**Prader-Willi Homes of Oconomowoc** (PWHO) specializes in providing residential services and supports to individuals diagnosed with Prader-Willi Syndrome (PWS). For over 35 years, PWHO has been nationally and internationally recognized by the PWS community for excellence in the therapeutic treatment and care for individuals diagnosed with PWS, and now supports more individuals diagnosed with PWS than any other residential provider in the world.

Prader-Willi Homes of Oconomowoc /
Admissions Director
P.O. Box 278
Dousman, WI 53118
262-569-4848
*http://www.pwho.com*

Writers of the Round Table Press
PO Box 511
Highland Park, IL 60035

| | |
|---|---|
| Illustration | NATHAN LUETH |
| Publisher | COREY MICHAEL BLAKE |
| Executive Editor | KATIE GUTIERREZ |
| Creative Director | DAVID CHARLES COHEN |
| Post Production | SUNNY DIMARTINO |
| Director of Operations | KRISTIN WESTBERG |
| Facts Keeper | MIKE WINICOUR |
| Front Cover Design | NATHAN LUETH, SUNNY DIMARTINO |
| Interior Design and Layout | SUNNY DIMARTINO |
| Last Looks | SUNNY DIMARTINO |
| Digital Publishing | SUNNY DIMARTINO |

Printed in the United States of America

First Edition: September 2014
10 9 8 7 6 5 4 3 2 1

**Library of Congress Cataloging-in-Publication Data**
Frisk, Debbie
Ultra-violet: one girl's prader-willi story / Debbie Frisk and Chelsea McCutchin with James G. Balestrieri.—1st ed. p. cm.
Print ISBN: 978-1-939418-70-8 Digital ISBN: 978-1-939418-71-5
Library of Congress Control Number: 2014915822
Number 9 in the series: The ORP Library
The ORP Library: Ultra-Violet

# Ultra-Violet

## ONE GIRL'S PRADER-WILLI STORY

THE ORP LIBRARY

ILLUSTRATED BY NATHAN LUETH

WRITTEN BY CHELSEA McCUTCHIN
DEBBIE FRISK

WITH JAMES G. BALESTRIERI

# Introduction

I have led Oconomowoc Residential Programs (ORP) for almost thirty years. We're a family of companies offering specialized services and care for children, adolescents, and adults with disabilities. Too often, when parents of children with disabilities try to find funding for programs like ours, they are bombarded by red tape, conflicting information, or no information at all, so they struggle blindly for years to secure an appropriate education. Meanwhile, home life, and the child's wellbeing, suffers. In cases when parents and caretakers have exhausted their options—and their hope—ORP is here to help. We felt it was time to offer parents a new, unexpected tool to fight back: stories that educate, empower, and inspire.

The original idea was to create a library of comic books that could empower families with information to reclaim their rights. We wanted to give parents and caretakers the information they need to advocate for themselves, as well as provide educators and therapists with a therapeutic tool. And, of course, we wanted to reach the children—to offer them a visual representation of their journey that would show that they aren't alone, nor are they wrong or "bad" for their differences.

What we found in the process of writing original stories for the comics is that these journeys are too long, too complex, to be contained within a standard comic. So what we are now creating is an ORP library of disabilities books—traditional books geared toward parents, caretakers, educators, and therapists, *and* comic books like this one that portray the world through the eyes of children with disabilities. Both styles of books share what we have learned while advocating for families over the years while also honestly highlighting their emotional journeys.

In an ideal situation, this companion children's book will be used therapeutically, to communicate directly with these amazing children, and to help support the work ORP and companies like ours are doing. These books are the best I have to offer and if they even help a handful of people the effort will have been worth it.

Sincerely,

*Jim Balestrieri*
*CEO, Oconomowoc Residential Programs*

MOST OF THE TIME, I WAS A NICE AND WELL-BEHAVED LITTLE GIRL. I ENJOYED PLAYING WITH MY BROTHERS, AND I LOVED MY PARENTS VERY MUCH.

BUT I ALWAYS FELT LIKE I WAS STARVING, NO MATTER HOW MUCH I ATE OR HOW BIG I GOT. AND WHENEVER MY PARENTS TRIED TO STOP ME FROM EATING, IT FELT LIKE THEY WERE TAKING AWAY MY ONLY LIFELINE.
I THREW TANTRUMS, I LASHED OUT, I SCREAMED, I SWORE AND HIT ANYONE WHO GOT BETWEEN ME AND FOOD.

# A Note About This Book

Prader-Willi Syndrome is a complex disorder that affects children, teens, and adults in different ways. The child with Prader-Willi Syndrome in this book struggles with physical, emotional, and behavioral challenges that require a therapeutic environment. At Prader-Willi Homes of Oconomowoc, we strive to build relationships with our clients and collaborate with their families to teach them skills that will contribute to healthier, safer, and happier lives. It is our hope that this book will add to your own understanding of the often-lonely journey of families experiencing these unique challenges—and gifts.

DO YOU KNOW HOW IT FEELS WHEN YOU'RE STARVING? WHEN YOU'RE SO HUNGRY THAT YOU'LL DO ANYTHING FOR FOOD? THAT YOU'LL DO *ANYTHING*?
LUKAS!!
MITCHELL!!
BIRTHDAY
GET DOWN HERE RIGHT NOW!
WHAT'S UP, MOM?
THESE SANDWICHES WERE SUPPOSED TO BE FOR VIOLET'S BIRTHDAY PARTY! WHAT WERE YOU THINKING?
IT WASN'T US!
IT'S TRUE, DEAR. WE'VE BEEN UPSTAIRS PLAYING VIDEO GAMES ALL AFTERNOON.
THEN WHO...?

NOW IMAGINE WHAT IT WOULD BE LIKE TO FEEL THAT WAY EVERY SECOND OF EVERY DAY.
VIOLET? VIOLET, WHERE ARE YOU?
THAT'S HOW I'VE FELT FOR AS LONG AS I CAN REMEMBER.
THERE YOU ARE! COME DOWN HERE, RIGHT NOW!
IF YOU DON'T COME DOWN, YOU'RE GOING TO SPEND THE AFTERNOON IN YOUR ROOM WHILE THE PARTY IS GOING ON! NO MORE SANDWICHES FOR YOU!
NO!

MY MOM WAS JUST WORRIED ABOUT ME. SHE WAS TRYING TO KEEP ME FROM MAKING MYSELF SICK.
NOOO -OOO!
CRACK!
BUT ALL I HEARD WAS THAT SOMEONE WAS GOING TO TAKE MY FOOD AWAY.
MUNCH* CHOMP*SMACK
VIOLET! STOP! YOU'LL CHOKE IF YOU KEEP EATING SO FAST!
I DIDN'T EVEN REALIZE THAT I BROKE MY ANKLE WHEN I JUMPED OFF THE REFRIGERATOR. IT DIDN'T HURT. AND ALL I COULD THINK ABOUT WAS HOW HUNGRY I WAS.

THAT WASN'T ALL, EITHER. AT SCHOOL, I WOULD STEAL FROM OTHER KIDS' LUNCHES, IF THE TEACHER WASN'T WATCHING.
I HID FOOD IN MY ROOM SO I WOULD HAVE SOMETHING TO EAT LATE AT NIGHT.
MOM AND DAD CAUGHT ME, BUT I COULDN'T SURRENDER. I HAD TO HAVE EVERY CRUMB.
...AND WHEN I WAS DONE WITH THAT, I WOULD SNEAK DOWN TO THE PANTRY FOR MORE.
THINKING FAST, I SHOVED AS MUCH AS I COULD IN MY MOUTH. THEY COULDN'T GET IT IF THEY COULDN'T REACH IT.
THE COOKIE GOT STUCK. MY FACE GOT HOT AND I COULDN'T BREATHE.
HK-* HK-* HK-* HK-*
DADDY GOT ME JUST IN TIME IN A HUG SO TIGHT IT HURT.

THINGS GOT SO BAD THAT MY MOM STARTED TAKING ME TO SEE DOCTORS.
YOU JUST HAVE A TOUGH LITTLE GIRL WHO LIKES TO EAT.
NONE OF THEM SEEMED TO HELP, OR REALLY EVEN THINK THAT ANYTHING WAS WRONG.
TRY FEEDING HER HEALTHIER FOODS AND GET HER SOME EXERCISE.
MOM TRIED SO HARD FOR ME. IT REALLY STRESSED HER OUT.
YOU CLEARLY FEEL GUILTY ABOUT BEING A WORKING MOTHER.

MOST OF THE TIME, I WAS A NICE AND WELL-BEHAVED LITTLE GIRL. I ENJOYED PLAYING WITH MY BROTHERS, AND I LOVED MY PARENTS VERY MUCH.
BUT I ALWAYS FELT LIKE I WAS STARVING, NO MATTER HOW MUCH I ATE OR HOW BIG I GOT. AND WHENEVER MY PARENTS TRIED TO STOP ME FROM EATING, IT FELT LIKE THEY WERE TAKING AWAY MY ONLY LIFELINE.
I THREW TANTRUMS, I LASHED OUT, I SCREAMED, I SWORE AND HIT ANYONE WHO GOT BETWEEN ME AND FOOD.
TO MAKE MATTERS WORSE, WHENEVER I GOT NERVOUS ABOUT SOMETHING, I WOULD PICK AT MY SCALP UNTIL IT WAS BLOODY.

MY DAD SCOURED THE INTERNET DAY AND NIGHT FOR CLUES ABOUT WHAT THE PROBLEM MIGHT BE. MOST OF THE TIME HE DIDN'T FIND ANYTHING, UNTIL...
HONEY! CHECK THIS OUT!
WHAT IS IT?
AN ARTICLE ABOUT A NEW GENETICS TEST FOR VIOLET. IT'S CALLED A FISH* TEST.
*FLUORESCENTS IN SITU HYBRIDIZATION
WHAT'S A FISH TEST?
DIDN'T WE ALREADY GIVE HER A GENETICS TEST?
YEAH, BUT THIS ONE COVERS MORE GROUND.
BASICALLY, IT CHECKS THE ENTIRE DNA FOR ANY ERRORS OR ABNORMALITIES. I THINK THAT COULD BRING US A STEP CLOSER TO FIGURING OUT WHAT'S GOING ON WITH VIOLET.
WHAT DO WE HAVE TO LOSE?

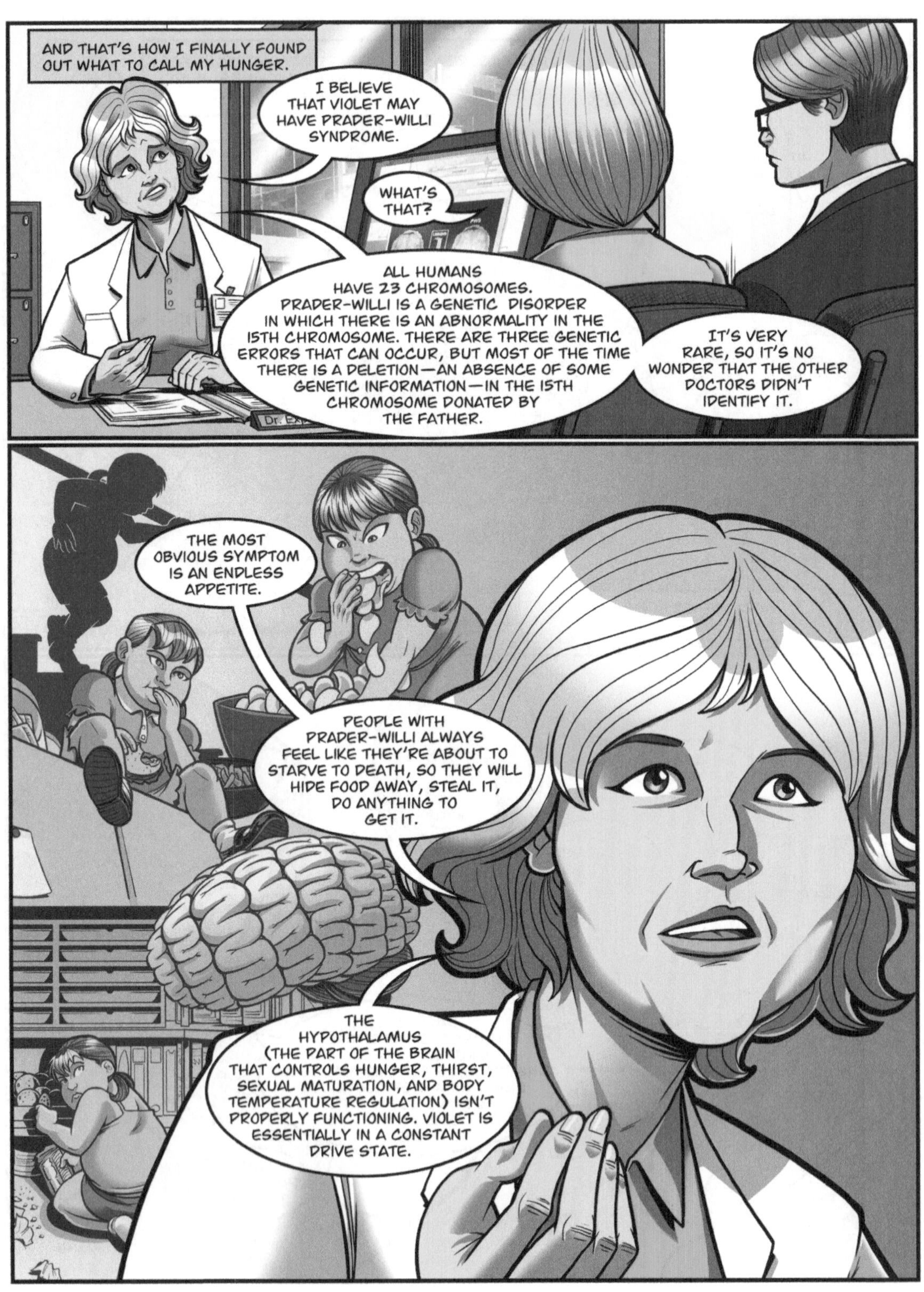
AND THAT'S HOW I FINALLY FOUND OUT WHAT TO CALL MY HUNGER.
I BELIEVE THAT VIOLET MAY HAVE PRADER-WILLI SYNDROME.
WHAT'S THAT?
ALL HUMANS HAVE 23 CHROMOSOMES. PRADER-WILLI IS A GENETIC DISORDER IN WHICH THERE IS AN ABNORMALITY IN THE 15TH CHROMOSOME. THERE ARE THREE GENETIC ERRORS THAT CAN OCCUR, BUT MOST OF THE TIME THERE IS A DELETION—AN ABSENCE OF SOME GENETIC INFORMATION—IN THE 15TH CHROMOSOME DONATED BY THE FATHER.
IT'S VERY RARE, SO IT'S NO WONDER THAT THE OTHER DOCTORS DIDN'T IDENTIFY IT.
THE MOST OBVIOUS SYMPTOM IS AN ENDLESS APPETITE.
PEOPLE WITH PRADER-WILLI ALWAYS FEEL LIKE THEY'RE ABOUT TO STARVE TO DEATH, SO THEY WILL HIDE FOOD AWAY, STEAL IT, DO ANYTHING TO GET IT.
THE HYPOTHALAMUS (THE PART OF THE BRAIN THAT CONTROLS HUNGER, THIRST, SEXUAL MATURATION, AND BODY TEMPERATURE REGULATION) ISN'T PROPERLY FUNCTIONING. VIOLET IS ESSENTIALLY IN A CONSTANT DRIVE STATE.

"DRIVE STATE"?
YES. IT MEANS SHE IS CONSTANTLY DRIVEN TO FIND FOOD.
NOT ONLY IS VIOLET CONSTANTLY HUNGRY, BUT SHE ALSO HAS A DECREASED METABOLISM THAT ONLY BURNS CALORIES AT A THIRD THE RATE OF A NORMAL PERSON.
Rx INSULIN
IF HER FOOD INTAKE ISN'T MANAGED, SHE COULD LITERALLY EAT HERSELF TO DEATH, OR SUFFER THE SAME HEALTH PROBLEMS THAT ANY OVERWEIGHT PERSON MIGHT FACE.
WHAT CAN WE DO?
IT MAY SOUND DRASTIC, BUT THE BEST COURSE OF ACTION IS TO LOCK UP ALL THE FOOD IN YOUR HOUSE, KEEP A STRICT SCHEDULE FOR MEAL TIMES, AND MAKE SURE SHE GETS EXERCISE EVERY DAY.
ALSO, IT IS VERY COMMON TO HAVE PSYCHOLOGICAL AND BEHAVIORAL ISSUES THAT COMPOUND THE PROBLEM CAUSED BY PW. I RECOMMEND TAKING HER TO SEE A PSYCHIATRIST AND SEEING IF SHE NEEDS MEDICATION.
I KNOW THIS SEEMS LIKE A LOT TO TAKE IN, BUT THERE ARE RESOURCES AVAILABLE TO YOU. THE PRADER-WILLI SYNDROME ASSOCIATION USA, FOR INSTANCE.
I'LL MAKE SURE YOU GET ALL THE INFORMATION YOU NEED BEFORE YOU LEAVE.

AND SO BEGAN MY NEW NORMAL. EVERYTHING IN THE KITCHEN HAD TO BE LOCKED UP AT ALL TIMES.

THE PSYCHIATRIST DIAGNOSED ME WITH OBSESSIVE COMPULSIVE DISORDER, ANXIETY, AND ATTENTION DEFICIT HYPERACTIVITY DISORDER, SO I STARTED TAKING MEDICATION.
M T W Th F S

MEALS HAPPENED AT THE EXACT SAME TIME EVERY DAY SO I NEVER HAD TO WORRY THAT MY PARENTS WOULD FORGET TO FEED ME.

AND MY BROTHER MITCHELL ATE LUNCH WITH ME AT SCHOOL EVERY DAY TO MAKE SURE THAT I WAS SAFE.
IT SOUNDS LIKE I WAS IN JAIL, BUT IT ACTUALLY MADE ME FEEL BETTER. I FELT LIKE MY FAMILY WAS LOOKING OUT FOR ME.

BUT, BY THE TIME I GOT TO HIGH SCHOOL, MITCHELL HAD GRADUATED AND WAS OFF TO COLLEGE.
THE SCHOOL ARRANGED FOR ME TO HAVE A "LUNCH BUDDY" INSTEAD.
TITANS

BUT SHE DIDN'T REALIZE HOW QUICK I COULD BE IF SHE WASN'T CONSTANTLY WATCHING ME.
TITANS
ZOOM

HEY!

WHAT DO YOU THINK YOU'RE DOING? YOU CAN'T JUST TAKE THINGS THAT DON'T BELONG TO YOU!

I DON'T CARE THAT YOU'RE A GIRL, OR A RETARD, OR WHATEVER. YOU'RE BEING DISRESPECTFUL.
...AND I DON'T HANDLE DISRESPECT WELL.
WHAT IS THE MEANING OF THIS!? BACK UP RIGHT NOW!

F@&# YOU, OLD LADY!
I WILL NOT STAND FOR THIS! YOUNG LADY, YOUR BEHAVIOR IS UNACCEPTABLE. YOU WILL FOLLOW ME TO THE OFFICE AT ONCE.
FORTUNATELY MY PARENTS WERE ABLE TO EXPLAIN PRADER-WILLI SYNDROME TO THE PRINCIPAL AND CONVINCED HER NOT TO EXPEL ME.
SHE DID WANT TO REVISIT MY INDIVIDUALIZED EDUCATION PLAN, BUT THAT TURNED OUT TO BE A GOOD THING...

...BECAUSE TWO YEARS LATER I GRADUATED FROM HIGH SCHOOL WITH THE REST OF MY CLASSMATES.
EXIT
WELL, I DIDN'T REALLY GRADUATE, BUT I WAS THE SPECIAL GUEST OF HONOR AT THE GRADUATION CEREMONY AND GOT A SPECIAL CERTIFICATE.
I KNOW I CAN BE HARD TO DEAL WITH SOMETIMES. I KNOW THAT PRADER-WILLI CAN BE A BURDEN ON OTHERS, TOO, NOT JUST ME...
...WHICH IS WHY I'M SO THANKFUL FOR THE PEOPLE WHO NEVER GAVE UP ON ME.

UNFORTUNATELY, PRADER-WILLI NEVER GOES AWAY, NO MATTER HOW WELL IT IS MANAGED. IT'S NOT A MATTER OF WILLPOWER, AND THE MEDICATIONS I WAS TAKING TO HELP MANAGE MY BEHAVIOR COULDN'T MAKE ME LESS HUNGRY.
THEY ONLY MADE ME REALLY, REALLY TIRED. SO MY FIRST DECISION AS AN ADULT WAS TO STOP TAKING MY MEDICATIONS.
MY PARENTS TOOK TURNS WATCHING ME DURING THE DAY, BUT I KNEW WHERE THEY HID THE KEY TO THE PANTRY. IT WAS EASY TO SWIPE IT AND SNEAK DOWN IN THE MIDDLE OF THE NIGHT.
HOCOLATE MILK
IT WAS ONLY A MATTER OF TIME BEFORE THEY STARTED NOTICING THE MISSING FOOD, THOUGH.

...BUT THEN I HAD ANOTHER IDEA.
UP ALL NITE
I POLISHED OFF MY FIRST BAG OF FOOD. AND THEN WENT BACK IN FOR MORE. THERE WAS NOTHING TO STOP ME. I COULD HAVE EATEN THE STORE OUT OF BUSINESS IF I HAD WANTED TO! THERE WAS JUST ONE PROBLEM...
I HAD RUN OUT OF MONEY.
HEY! WHAT ARE YOU DOING?

WHA—? NOTHING! SHOPPING!
LISTEN, I KNOW THAT YOU'RE TRYING TO TAKE THINGS. JUST PUT THEM BACK AND LEAVE OR I'LL HAVE TO CALL THE COPS.
I'M NOT STEALING! Y-YOU'RE STEALING!
JUST PUT IT BACK AND WE'LL BE FINE.
HEY!
NYAAGGHHH!!
I DIDN'T MEAN TO HURT ANYBODY. I WAS JUST DESPERATE FOR FOOD. FOOD THAT HAD BEEN THREATENED TO BE TAKEN AWAY.
...NOT EVEN SUPPOSED TO BE HERE, TODAY.

WHAT'S GOING ON IN HERE?
THERE'S SOMETHING WRONG WITH THIS GIRL! SHE'S JUST GOING **NUTS!**

MISS, I NEED YOU TO STAY WHERE YOU ARE AND KEEP YOUR HANDS WHERE I CAN SEE THEM.
POP
POP
POP

I WISH I COULD SAY THAT I MADE A DARING ESCAPE, BUT THAT WOULDN'T BE TRUE.

BECAUSE OF MY PRADER-WILLI AND SINCE IT WAS MY FIRST OFFENSE, THE POLICE LET ME OFF WITH A WARNING. BUT I HAD VIOLATED MY PARENTS' TRUST, AND THEY DIDN'T KNOW WHAT TO DO WITH ME.

MY DAD STARTED SLEEPING OUTSIDE MY BEDROOM DOOR. BUT THAT ONLY WORKED FOR SO LONG BEFORE ANOTHER PROBLEM STARTED.
DEAR! WHAT ARE YOU DOING!?
HNG—* WHA...?
WHERE'S VIOLET?
SHE'S NOT IN THE KITCHEN AND THE PANTRY'S STILL LOCKED.
THE ALARM IS STILL ON, TOO. SHE'S GOT TO BE IN THE HOUSE SOMEWHERE.
I'M NOT HERE.
I HAD A MOSQUITO BITE AND I COULDN'T SCRATCH IT ENOUGH.

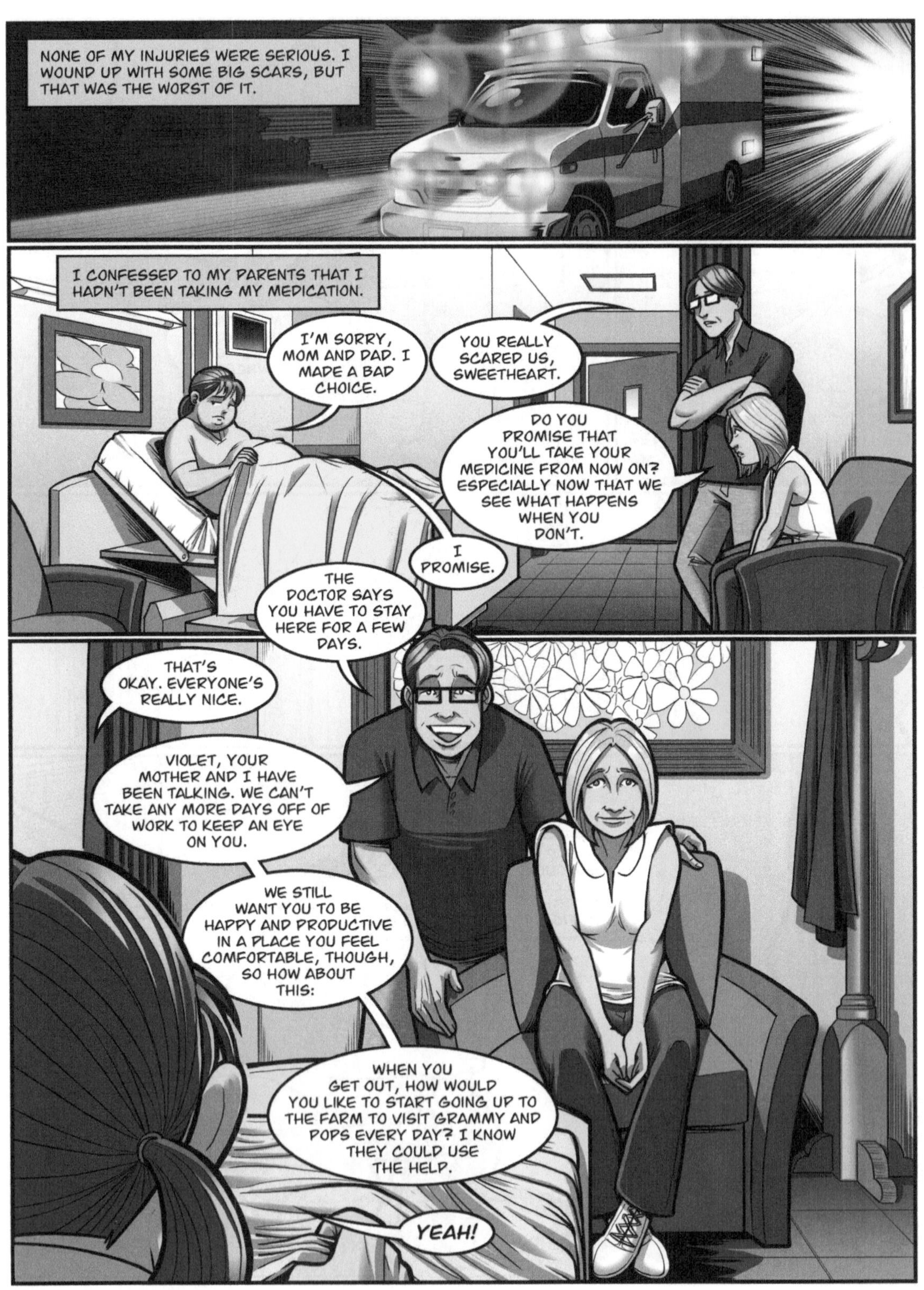
NONE OF MY INJURIES WERE SERIOUS. I WOUND UP WITH SOME BIG SCARS, BUT THAT WAS THE WORST OF IT.
I CONFESSED TO MY PARENTS THAT I HADN'T BEEN TAKING MY MEDICATION.
I'M SORRY, MOM AND DAD. I MADE A BAD CHOICE.
YOU REALLY SCARED US, SWEETHEART.
DO YOU PROMISE THAT YOU'LL TAKE YOUR MEDICINE FROM NOW ON? ESPECIALLY NOW THAT WE SEE WHAT HAPPENS WHEN YOU DON'T.
I PROMISE.
THE DOCTOR SAYS YOU HAVE TO STAY HERE FOR A FEW DAYS.
THAT'S OKAY. EVERYONE'S REALLY NICE.
VIOLET, YOUR MOTHER AND I HAVE BEEN TALKING. WE CAN'T TAKE ANY MORE DAYS OFF OF WORK TO KEEP AN EYE ON YOU.
WE STILL WANT YOU TO BE HAPPY AND PRODUCTIVE IN A PLACE YOU FEEL COMFORTABLE, THOUGH, SO HOW ABOUT THIS:
WHEN YOU GET OUT, HOW WOULD YOU LIKE TO START GOING UP TO THE FARM TO VISIT GRAMMY AND POPS EVERY DAY? I KNOW THEY COULD USE THE HELP.
YEAH!

MY GRANDPARENTS LIVED ABOUT 45 MINUTES AWAY BY COMMUTER TRAIN. DAD RODE WITH ME THE WHOLE WAY THERE, DROPPED ME OFF, THEN PICKED ME UP IN THE EVENING TO TAKE ME HOME.
GOOD THING FOR HIM THE TRAIN HAD WIFI.
POPS!
HIYA, PURPLE. READY TO GO?
YOU BET! WHERE'S GRAMMY?
GETTING EVERYTHING READY FOR YOU. I THINK SHE MAY HAVE SOME CRAFTS UP HER SLEEVE TODAY.
ARE WE GOING TO KNIT?
YOU'LL JUST HAVE TO WAIT AND SEE.
GRAMMY AND POP WERE SWEET, BUT THEY DIDN'T MISS A TRICK. MOM AND DAD HAD FILLED THEM IN ON ALL MY ESCAPADES.
GRAMMY, DADDY WANTED ME TO TELL YOU THAT HE DIDN'T HAVE TIME TO FEED ME BREAKFAST THIS MORNING. HE WANTED TO KNOW IF I COULD HAVE BREAKFAST HERE.
VIOLET, YOUR DADDY TOLD ME THAT HE FED YOU BREAKFAST BEFORE YOU GOT ON THE TRAIN. NOW YOU'RE NOT GOING TO TELL ME STORIES, ARE YOU? I WON'T PUT UP WITH IT.

...UNFORTUNATELY, I DIDN'T MISS A TRICK, EITHER.

GRAMMY HAD DOZED OFF ONE AFTERNOON, POPS WAS OUT ON THE TRACTOR, AND I WAS BORED AND LOOKING FOR SOMETHING TO DO.

I HAD WANDERED INTO THE BEDROOM AND I WAS THINKING OF TRYING ON SOME OF GRAMMY'S MAKEUP, WHEN I SAW IT...

I TOOK A LITTLE BIT AT A TIME FROM GRAMMY AND, OVER THE COURSE OF SIX WEEKS, IT TURNED INTO QUITE A BIT. AFTER THAT I JUST HAD TO WAIT FOR AN OPPORTUNITY.
WE HAVE A LITTLE SURPRISE FOR YOU, VIOLET. I HAVE TO WORK LATE TOMORROW, AND SINCE YOU'VE BEEN DOING SO WELL AT GRAMMY AND POP'S, WHAT DO YOU SAY TO RIDING THE TRAIN HOME, YOURSELF?
YES! THAT WOULD BE WONDERFUL!
YOU'RE A GROWN LADY WITH A CELL PHONE. I'LL PICK YOU UP AT 7:30. CAN WE TRUST YOU TO DO THIS?
YES! OF COURSE! I PROMISE.
8:45 PM
IT WAS THE CHANCE I'D BEEN WAITING FOR.
HI GRAMMY, IT'S ME.
NO, I STILL HAVEN'T SEEN HER. ARE YOU SURE SHE GOT ON THE RIGHT TRAIN?
. . .
OKAY, THANKS. I'LL LET YOU KNOW IF I FIND HER.
IHOW
END

VIOLET! WE WERE SO WORRIED! WHERE HAVE YOU BEEN?
HI MOM! I'M HAVING DINNER!
CHECK IT OUT! ALL YOU CAN EAT WAFFLES!
YOU CAN ONLY GET TWO PIECES OF BACON OR SAUSAGE AND TWO SCRAMBLED EGGS, BUT THEY KEEP THE WAFFLES COMING UNTIL YOU SAY STOP.
I HAVEN'T SAID STOP.
VIOLET, HOW WERE YOU GOING TO PAY FOR THIS? YOU DON'T HAVE ANY MONEY.
I WORK FOR GRAMMY AND POPS. THEY GIVE ME MONEY.
THAT'S NOT TRUE. THEY KNOW BETTER THAN THAT. THEY—
I'M AN ADULT! I HAVE A JOB TO TAKE CARE OF GRAMMY AND POPS DURING THE DAY! I TAKE CARE OF EVERYTHING! IT'S FINE THAT I WANTED TO HAVE A LITTLE DINNER ALONE!
VIOLET, I—
#@&% OFF, MOM! I'M DONE WITH THIS AND I'M DONE WITH YOU! I HATE YOUR GUTS!
VIOLET!

HONEY, IT'S ME! I FOUND VIOLET IN A WAFFLE HOUSE! SHE YELLED AT ME AND RAN OUT AND NOW SHE'S GONE! I DON'T KNOW WHAT TO DO!
I'M GOING TO CALL THE POLICE. STAY THERE IN CASE SHE COMES BACK. I'LL COME UP TOO. IT'LL BE OKAY.

...AND THAT WAS THE SECOND TIME THE POLICE BROUGHT ME BACK TO MY FAMILY.
MY PARENTS LOVED ME VERY MUCH, AND WANTED TO TAKE THE BEST CARE OF ME THAT THEY COULD. BUT IT WAS BECOMING CLEAR THAT THEY MIGHT NEED MORE HELP THAN THEY THOUGHT.

MOM AND DAD FOUND A RESIDENTIAL CARE FACILITY IN TOWN THAT WAS STARTING UP ITS OWN PRADER-WILLI CARE PROGRAM.
I DON'T THINK THEY FULLY UNDERSTOOD WHAT THEY WERE DEALING WITH, THOUGH.
MY ROOMMATE, JENNIFER, HAD AUTISM AND HER MOTHER SENT HER CARE PACKAGES OF COOKIES AND CANDY ALL THE TIME.
JENNIFER SHARED WITH ME, EVEN THOUGH I TOOK MORE THAN MY PART WHEN SHE WAS ASLEEP. PLUS, NOBODY MADE ME EXERCISE! THEY DIDN'T EVEN LOCK THE KITCHENS AT NIGHT!
1:00 AM
AFTER I GAINED TWENTY-FIVE POUNDS IN TWO WEEKS, MY PARENTS DECIDED THAT WASN'T THE PLACE FOR ME.
IT WAS PROBABLY A GOOD PLACE FOR KIDS WITH OTHER SPECIAL NEEDS, THEY JUST DIDN'T KNOW ENOUGH ABOUT PRADER-WILLI.

MY PARENTS KEPT LOOKING FOR OTHER PLACES FOR ME TO LIVE. IN MY MIND, THAT COULD ONLY MEAN ONE THING:
WHY ARE YOU TRYING TO GET RID OF ME?
WE WOULD NEVER TRY TO GET RID OF YOU, SWEETIE. WE'RE JUST TRYING TO FIND A PLACE WHERE YOU CAN BE HAPPY.
I CAN'T BE HAPPY! I DIDN'T ASK TO HAVE PRADER-WILLI! I DON'T WANT TO BE THIS WAY! I WANT TO GO TO COLLEGE. I WANT TO GET MARRIED AND HAVE BABIES. I WANT TO BE PRETTY AND BE A GROWN-UP LIKE LUKE AND MITCH.
YOU ARE PRETTY, AND YOU ARE GROWN UP. THIS COULD BE THE PLACE WHERE YOU'RE ALLOWED TO DO ALL OF THAT. THIS IS A FACILITY DESIGNED FOR PEOPLE WHO DIDN'T ASK FOR PRADER-WILLI. YOU COULD HAVE A JOB, MAKE FRIENDS, AND LIVE IN A SUPPORTIVE ENVIRONMENT. NOTHING IS FOR SURE YET, VIOLET. WE'RE ALL GOING TO LOOK AT THIS PLACE TOMORROW. WE WILL ALL DECIDE IF YOU GO THERE. NOT LIKE LAST TIME.
*SNIFFLE* R-REALLY?
I PROMISE. YOU DON'T HAVE TO STAY IF YOU DON'T LIKE IT.

AND THAT WAS HOW WE CAME TO PRADER-WILLI HOMES OF OCONOMOWOC.
HI! I'M MARILYN! THIS IS LAUREN, OUR CLINICAL COORDINATOR, AND KELLY, THE HOUSE MANAGER FOR THE HOME THAT WE'LL BE LOOKING AT TODAY. IT'S SO NICE TO FINALLY MEET YOU ALL!
YOU MUST BE VIOLET. YOU'RE EVEN PRETTIER THAN YOUR MOM DESCRIBED.
TH-THANK YOU.
VI, WOULD YOU MIND TAKING THE TOUR WITH KELLY WHILE DAD AND I GO BACK TO LAUREN'S OFFICE FOR A BIT?
YOU'RE NOT GOING TO TALK ABOUT ME ARE YOU!?
ONLY BORING STUFF. IN THE MEANTIME, KELLY'S GOING TO SHOW YOU AROUND TO SEE IF YOU LIKE IT HERE. OKAY?
OKAY...

IS THERE ENOUGH FOOD HERE?
GREAT QUESTION, VIOLET.
HERE AT PWHO, WE ALL EAT TOGETHER AND MAKE SMART FOOD CHOICES THAT WILL HELP US BECOME HEALTHY. MORE IMPORTANTLY, WE HAVE A LOT OF FUN HERE! WE GO TO MOVIES, GO BOWLING, AND HAVE SOCIALS WITH DANCING SO THAT EVERYONE CAN BE TOGETHER AND HAVE A NICE TIME.
OUR RESIDENTS GET FREE TIME IN THE AFTERNOONS TO WORK ON THINGS THAT ARE IMPORTANT TO EACH OF THEM. WE'RE MORE THAN JUST A "HOUSE." WE'RE ALSO A FAMILY THAT HAS A REALLY GOOD TIME TOGETHER.
THE RESIDENTS AND STAFF ARE AT WORK RIGHT NOW, BUT WE CAN LOOK AROUND A BIT.
AT *WORK*?
THAT'S RIGHT! A LOT OF OUR RESIDENTS HAVE JOBS IN TOWN.
AND EVERYONE WHO LIVES HERE HAS PRADER-WILLI?
YUP! OUR GOAL HERE IS TO GIVE PEOPLE WITH PRADER-WILLI THE BEST OPPORTUNITIES POSSIBLE. WE ALSO HAVE FUN ACTIVITIES FOR OUR RESIDENTS, LIKE SPECIAL OLYMPICS SPORTS AND MOVIE NIGHTS. CHECK IT OUT!

OUR DAILY SCHEDULE IS POSTED SO YOU ALWAYS KNOW WHAT TO EXPECT.
WE START THE DAY WITH BREAKFAST, AND I COME DOWN TO THE TABLE AND TALK TO EVERYONE IN THE MORNING.
AFTER BREAKFAST, OUR RESIDENTS GO TO WORK.
AFTER WORK I HAVE A CHAT WITH RESIDENTS TO MAKE SURE EVERYTHING'S GOING OKAY, AND EVERYONE HAS TIME TO DO CHORES OR SHOPPING.
AFTER THAT WE HAVE SPORTS, OR WE ALL GO FOR A WALK.
AND IN THE EVENING, WE TRY TO DO FUN THINGS, LIKE GO BOWLING, WATCH MOVIES, OR JUST RELAX.

CHERISH
PERFECT! LOOKS LIKE SOME OF OUR RESIDENTS ARE JUST GETTING HOME FROM WORK. WOULD YOU LIKE TO MEET THEM?
SURE, I G—

HI! I'M STEPHANIE! ARE YOU COMING TO LIVE WITH US? DO YOU HAVE PRADER-WILLI?
Y-YEAH. YOU TOO, RIGHT?
YEP. I JUST CAME BACK FROM WORK. I WORK IN A FACTORY. I CHECK PACKAGES BEFORE THEY ARE MAILED OUT. I LOVE MY JOB, BUT TODAY I GOT MAD. DO YOU GET MAD SOMETIMES?

SOMETIMES I GET MAD. I TRY NOT TO, BUT I CAN'T HELP IT.
ARE YOU GOING TO LIVE HERE? I DON'T HAVE A ROOMMATE ANYMORE, SO IF YOU LIVE HERE, YOU'LL ROOM WITH ME! YOU'D BE HAPPY HERE. DO YOU LIKE TO WATCH TV? I DO. WE'LL BE BEST FRIENDS!
I DON'T KNOW. I'VE NEVER HAD A BEST FRIEND BEFORE.
YOU DO NOW.

VIOLET, YOUR PARENTS ARE HERE TO PICK YOU UP.
WHAT DO YOU SAY, KIDDO? DO YOU LIKE THIS PLACE?

FOUR WEEKS LATER...
I LOVE IT HERE!
THAT'S WONDERFUL, VI! I'M GLAD TO SEE THAT YOU'RE HAPPY.
I AM! I FEEL LIKE I GET TO BE AN ADULT HERE.
WHAT DOES THAT MEAN TO YOU?
I GET TO GO TO WORK EVERY MORNING.
I LIVE WITH MY FRIENDS, JUST LIKE MY BROTHERS AT COLLEGE. I'M THE YOUNGEST AND ONLY GIRL IN MY FAMILY, SO EVERYONE ALWAYS WANTED TO BABY ME.
I ALWAYS KNEW I WAS DIFFERENT FROM MY BROTHERS, BUT I DIDN'T REALIZE HOW MUCH UNTIL THEY WENT TO COLLEGE AND I DIDN'T.
NO ONE WAS HAPPY WITH ME LIVING AT HOME. BUT HERE, I CAN DO THE THINGS THAT I KNOW I CAN DO!
IT'S EASIER TO MAKE GOOD CHOICES WHEN I FEEL LIKE I'M IMPORTANT.
YOU ARE IMPORTANT, VIOLET. DID YOU NOT FEEL IMPORTANT WITH YOUR PARENTS?
I KNOW I'M IMPORTANT TO MY PARENTS AND THAT THEY LOVE ME. THEY TELL ME ALL THE TIME. BUT, HERE, I'M IMPORTANT TO OTHER PEOPLE, TOO.
MY JOB IS IMPORTANT. IF I DON'T GO TO WORK, THE FACTORY CAN'T GET MY JOB DONE WITHOUT ME. MY FRIENDS ARE IMPORTANT. THEY LOVE ME.
I'M GLAD TO HEAR YOU'RE DOING WELL. WHAT ARE YOU LOOKING FORWARD TO?
I WANT TO LEARN HOW TO MAKE EVEN BETTER CHOICES. I WANT TO TURN OFF THE VOICE THAT TELLS ME I'M HUNGRY!
WE CAN WORK ON THAT, BUT THAT "VOICE" MIGHT NEVER GO AWAY. WHAT WE'RE TRYING TO DO HERE IS MANAGE YOUR RESPONSE TO THAT VOICE, AND THE SAFER YOU FEEL THE EASIER THAT WILL BE.
DO YOU FEEL SAFE HERE?
YES!
AWESOME! NOW, WHY DON'T WE GO GET READY FOR OUR WALK?

I REALLY WAS HAPPY AT PWHO. I HAD FRIENDS, FREEDOM, AND RESPONSIBILITIES.
ONE THING STILL BOTHERED ME, THOUGH...
I HAD ALWAYS WANTED TO BE PRETTY, BUT PEOPLE WITH PRADER-WILLI HAVE A "UNIQUE" APPEARANCE.
I WOULD NEVER BE CONSIDERED PRETTY OR LOOK LIKE THE GIRLS IN THE MAGAZINES.
IN MY MIND, MY LOOKS STOOD FOR EVERYTHING THAT PRADER-WILLI HAD RUINED IN MY LIFE, AND I HATED THEM.
MY EYES WERE TOO CLOSE TOGETHER, MY HAIR WAS BROWN AND FLAT.
THAT MADE ME SO MAD!
THE MORE I RUINED HOW I LOOKED, THE MADDER I GOT, AND THE MADDER I GOT, THE MORE I COULDN'T HELP PICKING AT MYSELF.
KNOCK-KNOCK, VIOLET!
I JUST WANTED TO CHECK AND MAKE SURE YOU WERE—
OH!

OH NO! VIOLET! WHAT HAPPENED?
I PULLED MY HAIR OUT. I JUST WANT TO BE PRETTY AND POPULAR AND HAVE A BOYFRIEND.
I JUST WANT TO HAVE FUN!

WHEN WE SPOKE EARLIER YOU SAID YOU WERE HAPPY.
I AM HAPPY. BUT ONLY AS HAPPY AS VIOLET CAN BE. I'M NOT AS HAPPY AS A PRETTY GIRL CAN BE. I'M NOT AS HAPPY AS SOMEONE WITHOUT PRADER-WILLI CAN BE.

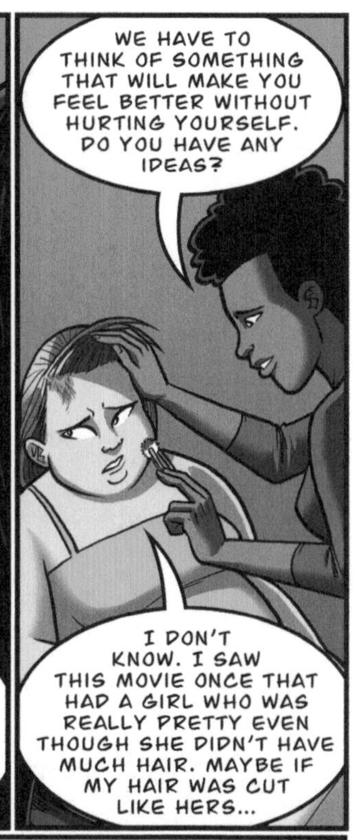
WE HAVE TO THINK OF SOMETHING THAT WILL MAKE YOU FEEL BETTER WITHOUT HURTING YOURSELF. DO YOU HAVE ANY IDEAS?
I DON'T KNOW. I SAW THIS MOVIE ONCE THAT HAD A GIRL WHO WAS REALLY PRETTY EVEN THOUGH SHE DIDN'T HAVE MUCH HAIR. MAYBE IF MY HAIR WAS CUT LIKE HERS...

I THINK YOU COULD LOOK LOVELY WITH THAT CUT. AND IF IT'S SHORT YOU WON'T BE ABLE TO PULL IT OUT AS EASILY. IF WE GET YOU THAT HAIRCUT, DO YOU PROMISE TO TALK TO SOMEONE THE NEXT TIME THAT YOU FEEL LIKE HURTING YOURSELF?
REALLY? I CAN GO TO THE SALON AND GET MY HAIR DONE, JUST LIKE MY MOM DOES?
YOU CERTAINLY MAY. I'LL TALK IT OVER WITH THE STAFF TOMORROW AND WE'LL MAKE AN APPOINTMENT. WOULD THAT MAKE YOU FEEL BETTER?

IT CERTAINLY DID.
THAT WASN'T ALL EITHER...

AAAAAAAAAAA

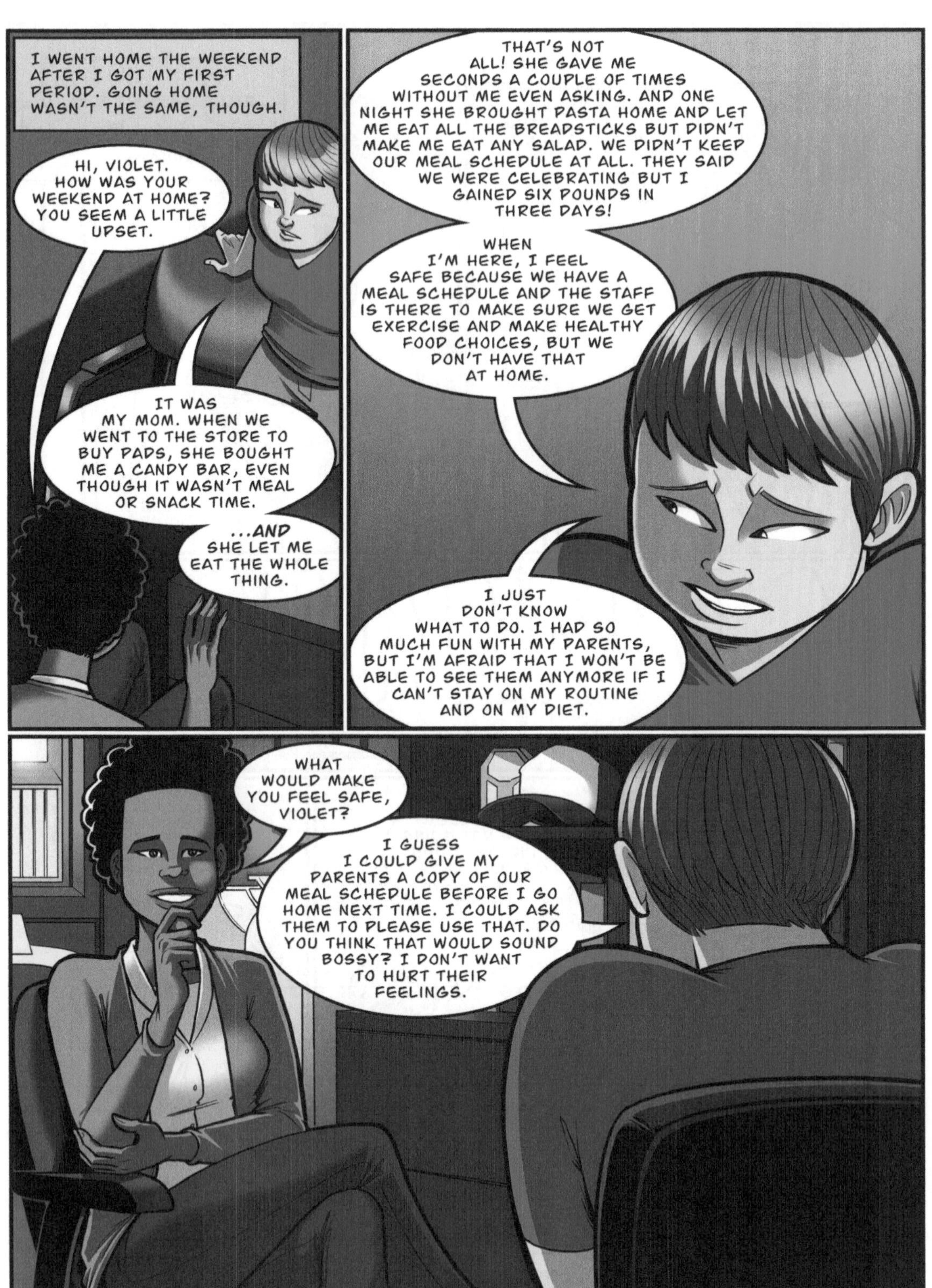
I WENT HOME THE WEEKEND AFTER I GOT MY FIRST PERIOD. GOING HOME WASN'T THE SAME, THOUGH.
HI, VIOLET. HOW WAS YOUR WEEKEND AT HOME? YOU SEEM A LITTLE UPSET.
IT WAS MY MOM. WHEN WE WENT TO THE STORE TO BUY PADS, SHE BOUGHT ME A CANDY BAR, EVEN THOUGH IT WASN'T MEAL OR SNACK TIME.
...AND SHE LET ME EAT THE WHOLE THING.
THAT'S NOT ALL! SHE GAVE ME SECONDS A COUPLE OF TIMES WITHOUT ME EVEN ASKING. AND ONE NIGHT SHE BROUGHT PASTA HOME AND LET ME EAT ALL THE BREADSTICKS BUT DIDN'T MAKE ME EAT ANY SALAD. WE DIDN'T KEEP OUR MEAL SCHEDULE AT ALL. THEY SAID WE WERE CELEBRATING BUT I GAINED SIX POUNDS IN THREE DAYS!
WHEN I'M HERE, I FEEL SAFE BECAUSE WE HAVE A MEAL SCHEDULE AND THE STAFF IS THERE TO MAKE SURE WE GET EXERCISE AND MAKE HEALTHY FOOD CHOICES, BUT WE DON'T HAVE THAT AT HOME.
I JUST DON'T KNOW WHAT TO DO. I HAD SO MUCH FUN WITH MY PARENTS, BUT I'M AFRAID THAT I WON'T BE ABLE TO SEE THEM ANYMORE IF I CAN'T STAY ON MY ROUTINE AND ON MY DIET.
WHAT WOULD MAKE YOU FEEL SAFE, VIOLET?
I GUESS I COULD GIVE MY PARENTS A COPY OF OUR MEAL SCHEDULE BEFORE I GO HOME NEXT TIME. I COULD ASK THEM TO PLEASE USE THAT. DO YOU THINK THAT WOULD SOUND BOSSY? I DON'T WANT TO HURT THEIR FEELINGS.

I BET YOU WON'T. YOU HAD TO TELL YOUR MOM THAT YOU NEEDED PADS, AND YOU HANDLED THAT WELL. THIS IS HOW ADULTS HANDLE THINGS, BY TALKING ABOUT THEM. LET'S GIVE THEM A CALL.
O-OKAY...

HI MOM. HI DAD.
HEY, HONEY!
HOW YA DOING, KIDDO?
I'M GOOD. BUT I WANTED TO TALK TO YOU ABOUT SOMETHING...
CALLING...

WHEN I GOT BACK HERE I REALIZED I HAD GAINED SIX POUNDS OVER THE WEEKEND.
WHEN I LIVED AT HOME WITH YOU, WE HAD OUR MEALS PLANNED OUT. NOW THAT I LIVE AT PWHO, WE HAVE OUR MEALS PLANNED OUT EVEN MORE. WHEN I CAME HOME LAST WEEKEND, WE DIDN'T HAVE OUR MEALS PLANNED AND I ATE MORE THAN WAS HEALTHY.
BEFORE I COME HOME NEXT TIME, I'D LIKE TO GIVE YOU A COPY OF OUR MEAL SCHEDULE. I THINK STICKING TO MY DIET AS MUCH AS POSSIBLE WOULD REALLY HELP ME OUT.

OH SWEETIE! WE'RE SO SORRY!
WE WERE SO EXCITED TO HANG OUT WITH YOU THAT WE BENT THE RULES WHILE YOU WERE HERE. WE MADE BAD CHOICES. WE DIDN'T MEAN TO DISRUPT YOUR DIET.
IF STICKING TO YOUR SCHEDULE WHILE YOU'RE AT HOME WILL MAKE YOU FEEL SAFE, THEN OF COURSE WE'LL DO IT.

I WAS SURPRISED AT HOW EASY IT WAS! I DIDN'T REALIZE UNTIL THAT MOMENT HOW MUCH THINGS HAD CHANGED SINCE I MOVED TO PWHO.
MOST IMPORTANTLY, I LEARNED THAT I COULD USE MY WORDS TO MAKE A POINT AND THAT I DIDN'T HAVE TO MELT DOWN WHEN I HAD A PROBLEM.

UNFORTUNATELY, THAT WASN'T ALWAYS A LESSON I REMEMBERED.
HEY! WHO'S IN THERE!? IT'S MY BIRTHDAY! I WAS SCHEDULED TO HAVE THE BATHROOM FIRST!
I GOT HERE FIRST! IT'S ONLY FAIR!
GWEN!? YOU'RE SUCH A SORRY @!#%$!! YOU'RE ALWAYS TAKING THINGS AWAY FROM OTHER PEOPLE!
WHAT'S GOING ON, VIOLET?
IT'S MY BIRTHDAY AND I WAS SUPPOSED TO HAVE THE SHOWER FIRST! GWEN GOT IN BEFORE ME AND NOW SHE'S GOING TO USE UP ALL THE HOT WATER! IT'S NOT FAIR!
YOU'RE RIGHT, IT'S NOT FAIR. I'LL TALK TO GWEN ABOUT THE SCHEDULE, BUT FOR NOW YOU NEED TO CALM DOWN.
IT'S TOO LATE! MY WHOLE BIRTHDAY IS ALREADY RUINED! I WOULDN'T EXPECT YOU TO UNDERSTAND, WENDY! YOU'RE A @!#%$!,TOO!

VIOLET? WHAT'S THE MATTER?

GWEN TOOK THE FIRST SHOWER WHEN I WAS SUPPOSED TO HAVE IT. IT'S MY BIRTHDAY, AND IT'S JUST NOT FAIR!

IT'S **NOT** FAIR, BUT WHAT'S SOMETHING THAT WE TALK ABOUT A LOT?

LIFE'S NOT FAIR?

NO, I'VE NEVER SAID THAT.

WHEN THINGS AREN'T FAIR, WE USE OUR WORDS TO TALK ABOUT ***WHY*** WE FEEL THINGS ARE UNFAIR. GWEN OWES YOU AN APOLOGY, BUT YOU ALSO OWE HER AND WENDY ONE FOR THE WAY THAT YOU TALKED TO THEM.

BUT IT WASN'T FAIR.

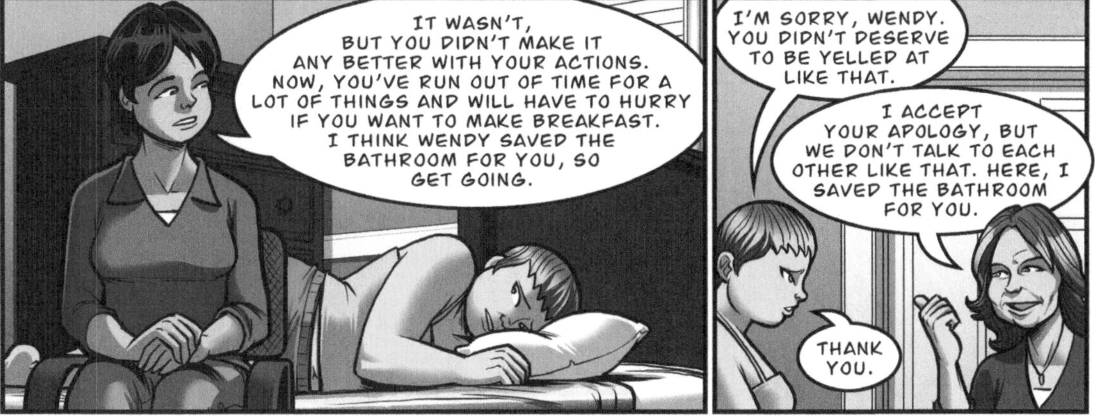

LATER, AFTER MY SHOWER...
GOOD MORNING EVERYBODY! AND HAPPY TWENTY-FIRST BIRTHDAY TO VIOLET!
I'M SORRY, GWEN.
ME TOO.
WE ALL HAVE BIRTHDAYS, AND WE SPEND THE DAY CELEBRATING THAT WE'VE BEEN ALIVE ANOTHER YEAR.
TODAY VIOLET IS TWENTY-ONE. SHE IS GETTING OLDER, AS WE ALL ARE. WHAT DOES IT MEAN TO GET OLDER?
WHEN I GET OLDER, I'M GOING TO MEET A BOY AND GET MARRIED!
LET'S STAY IN THE PRESENT, GWEN. WE DISCUSSED THAT BEFORE. WE NEED TO BE IN THE HERE AND NOW TO REALLY ENJOY OURSELVES.
BUT I'VE ALREADY STARTED PLANNING MY WEDDING. IT'S THE MOST IMPORTANT DAY OF A GIRL'S LIFE!
WHEN I WAS SHOPPING, I BOUGHT A BRIDAL MAGAZINE! I PICKED OUT THE WEDDING DRESS AND BRIDESMAIDS DRESSES I WOULD REALLY LIKE IF I GOT MARRIED!
IN MY SISTER'S WEDDING, I WORE A BEAUTIFUL DRESS. I DANCED WITH MY DAD, AND HE TOLD ME THAT I WAS A PRINCESS!
IT IS A LOT OF FUN TO DRESS UP AND GO TO PARTIES. WHEN WE WERE LITTLE KIDS, WEDDINGS MAY HAVE SEEMED BORING, BUT NOW THEY ARE EXCITING. THAT'S A GOOD EXAMPLE OF GETTING OLDER. THANKS, GWEN.

YOU DON'T UNDERSTAND!
I AM GETTING MARRIED AND THERE'S GOING TO BE A HUGE PARTY! WE'RE GOING TO HAVE A BUFFET AND WEDDING CAKE, AND PICTURES AND A DJ!
GWEN, WE TALKED ABOUT THIS. DO YOU REMEMBER? PLANNING PARTIES IS A LOT OF FUN, BUT HAVING A BIG WEDDING ISN'T REALLY A GOOD USE OF YOUR TIME RIGHT NOW.
BUT— BUT... WHAT IF I MEET THE PERFECT MAN? PRADER-WILLI IS SO RARE THAT IF I CAN BEAT THE ODDS AND HAVE THAT, COULDN'T I BEAT THEM AGAIN?
YOU'RE A WONDERFUL GIRL WITH A VERY FULL LIFE ALREADY, GWEN. LOVE IS A GREAT THING, BUT IT'S NOT EVERYTHING.
WE ALL HAVE GOOD FRIENDS. WE HAVE GOOD JOBS. WE'RE ALL VERY HAPPY THAT YOU'RE HERE.
TEE-HEE *GIGGLE* SNRF—*!
YOU'RE SUCH AN IDIOT, PETER! YOU'RE JUST JEALOUS! I'M A WOMAN AND YOU'LL ALWAYS BE A CHILD!

GWEN, PETER WAS MEAN FOR LAUGHING AT YOU, BUT GETTING MAD AT HIM BACK WON'T MAKE IT BETTER. YOU HAVE TO FORGIVE HIM, LIKE YOU FORGAVE ME FOR BEING MEAN THIS MORNING.
KELLY, I DON'T KNOW WHY VIOLET IS TRYING TO BE GOOD IN FRONT OF YOU. LAST NIGHT I SAW HER EAT HER DINNER WAY TOO FAST.
LIAR! I DID NOT!
PLEASE CALM DOWN, VI.
PETER, WE DON'T NEED TO TATTLE ON EACH OTHER. WE ONLY NEED TO TELL SOMEONE IF ONE OF OUR FRIENDS IS HURTING THEMSELVES OR SOMEONE ELSE. IF YOU WERE WORRIED ABOUT VIOLET EATING TOO FAST LAST NIGHT, AS HER FRIEND, YOU SHOULD HAVE SAID SOMETHING TO HER.
VIOLET, WOULD YOU SHOW EVERYONE HOW YOU WOULD APPROACH ME IF YOU THOUGHT I WAS EATING TOO FAST?
KELLY, I'M YOUR FRIEND AND I'M WORRIED ABOUT YOU. I SEE THAT YOU'RE EATING PRETTY FAST, AND I DON'T WANT YOU TO CHOKE.
VERY GOOD, VIOLET. THANKS FOR CARING ABOUT ME.
DOES EVERYONE HAVE A BETTER UNDERSTANDING OF HOW WE SHOULD TALK TO OUR FRIENDS?
MY TWENTY-FIRST BIRTHDAY HAD A ROUGH START, BUT IT ALL TURNED OUT WELL.
I WAS PROUD TO BE A GOOD EXAMPLE TO MY FRIENDS, I GOT TO TALK TO MY PARENTS AND BROTHERS ON THE PHONE, AND I EVEN GOT A BIRTHDAY BROWNIE AFTER DINNER!

...AND I HAD EXCITING NEW INTERESTS.
WHO IS THAT? HE'S GORGEOUS!
I THINK HIS NAME IS DEREK. HE JUST TRANSFERRED TO ANOTHER PWHO HOUSE.
HI! I'M VIOLET. I'M GLAD YOU MOVED HERE! IT'S A LOT OF FUN.
UH, THANKS. AH'M DEREK. AH'M FROM TENNESSEE.
WANT TO WALK WITH ME?
SURE.
YOU TALK FUNNY. I LIKE IT. IS IT BECAUSE YOU'RE FROM TENNESSEE?
AH GUESS. AH THINK YOU TALK FUNNY TOO.
NO WAY! DO YOU HAVE A GIRLFRIEND?
I DID AT THE LAST PLACE I LIVED, BUT NOT ANYMORE. DO YOU WANT TO BE MY GIRLFRIEND?
SURE!
PWHO RESIDENTS ARE ONLY ALLOWED TO HAVE GIRL-FRIENDS AND BOY-FRIENDS WHO LIVE IN OTHER HOUSES, SO DEREK WAS PERFECT.
I WAS SO EXCITED! A BOYFRIEND! FOR ME!
...AND WE'RE TOTALLY IN LOVE! WE'LL PROBABLY GET MARRIED!
MAYBE WE WON'T GET MARRIED, BUT WE'LL BE TOGETHER FOREVER!
YOUR RELATIONSHIP IS STILL VERY NEW. MAKE SURE YOU KNOW HIM WELL BEFORE YOU COMMIT YOURSELF TO BEING IN LOVE WITH HIM FOREVER. ENJOY THE WAY THINGS ARE NOW, BUT BE AWARE THAT SOMETIMES RELATIONSHIPS END AND IT CAN BE PAINFUL.

KELLY WAS LOOKING OUT FOR ME. AND IT TURNED OUT THAT SHE WAS RIGHT TO DO SO.
DEREK AND VIOLET, COME ON, GUYS!
KISSES ARE WONDERFUL, BUT LET'S SEPARATE A LITTLE.
DEREK, PATRICIA ASKED US TO STOP. I DON'T WANT TO GET IN TROUBLE.
YOU DON'T PUSH YOUR GIRLFRIEND, DEREK! I'M BREAKING UP WITH YOU! I NEVER WANT TO SEE YOU AGAIN!
MY HEART WAS BROKEN. I REALLY THOUGHT DEREK AND I WOULD BE TOGETHER FOREVER.
KELLY AND I CALLED MY PARENTS AND TALKING TO THEM MADE ME FEEL BETTER.
IT STILL HURT FOR A WHILE, THOUGH.

BEFORE I KNEW IT, IT WAS THE MOST WONDERFUL TIME OF THE YEAR, AND I WENT HOME AGAIN FOR CHRISTMAS.
WAKE UP, EVERYBODY! IT'S CHRISTMAS!
SANTA CAME! SANTA BROUGHT US PRESENTS! EVERYONE GETS A PRESENT!
EVERYTHING REALLY WAS WONDERFUL. LUKAS AND MITCHELL HAD BOTH GOTTEN MARRIED, AND MITCHELL'S WIFE WAS GOING TO HAVE A BABY! I WAS SO EXCITED TO BE AUNTIE VIOLET!
EVERYONE WAS SO HAPPY! IT SEEMED LIKE SO LONG AGO THAT MY PRADER-WILLI HAD CAUSED SO MANY PROBLEMS.
IN FACT, IT HAD BEEN SO LONG...

...THAT MY PARENTS WERE OUT OF PRACTICE.
WHAT'S GOING ON, VI? YOU'VE BEEN GONE FOR, LIKE, TEN MIN—
MOM! DAD! COME QUICK!!
*GASP*— HRR— RRK—*!
I VERY NEARLY CHOKED TO DEATH ON CHRISTMAS DAY. I COULDN'T BELIEVE IT! WHAT A TERRIBLE THING THAT WOULD HAVE BEEN TO DO TO MY FAMILY!

WHAT'S MORE, IT WAS A REMINDER THAT PRADER-WILLI SYNDROME WILL NEVER GO AWAY. IT WILL BE WITH ME ALL MY LIFE.
WHEN I WAS FORTY, I BROKE MY LEG PLAYING BASKETBALL ON MY BIRTHDAY. THE NURSE AT THE HOSPITAL DIDN'T KNOW ANYTHING ABOUT PRADER-WILLI, SO, WHILE MY STAFF WAS IN THE BATHROOM, I ORDERED FIVE WHOLE PLATES OF FOOD FROM THE KITCHEN!
I HAD EATEN A LOT MORE THAN I SHOULD HAVE BEFORE I WAS CAUGHT.
BUT FOR THE MOST PART, THE TWENTY YEARS OF MY LIFE AT PRADER-WILLI HOMES OF OCONOMOWOC HAVE BEEN HAPPY AND FULFILLING.
I HAVE A JOB I ENJOY. I HAVE FRIENDS I LIKE AND WHO LIKE ME. I AM A FUNCTIONING MEMBER OF SOCIETY.
VIOLET
BEST OF ALL, PEOPLE GET TO SEE THE REAL ME, THAT I AM A PERSON, AND NOT JUST A DISABILITY WITH A PERSON ATTACHED TO IT.

THE HARD PART ABOUT GETTING OLDER, IS THAT OTHER PEOPLE GET OLDER TOO.
HEY, VI, CAN I TALK TO YOU IN MY OFFICE FOR A FEW MINUTES?
BUT LAUREN, I'M GOING TO BE LATE FOR WORK.
DON'T WORRY ABOUT THAT. WE HAVE SOMETHING IMPORTANT TO TALK ABOUT.

LUKAS! EMILY! WHAT A SURPRISE! AM I GOING HOME WITH YOU TODAY?
YES, VIOLET. IT'S NOT A VACATION, THOUGH.

...MOM PASSED AWAY YESTERDAY. YOU'RE COMING HOME TO BE WITH US AS WE LAY HER TO REST.
SHE... DIED?
DOES THAT MEAN SHE'S IN HEAVEN?
VIOLET

IT DOES.
ARE YOU SAD?
I'M *VERY* SAD. DO YOU HAVE ANY QUESTIONS?
IS IT OKAY IF I CRY AT HOME?
YES. IT'S OKAY TO CRY IF YOU NEED TO. YOU CAN HAVE ANY REACTION THAT YOU FEEL, AS LONG AS YOU DON'T HURT YOURSELF OR ANYONE ELSE.

I DIDN'T CRY AT ALL WHILE I WAS HOME FOR MOM'S FUNERAL. EVERYONE WAS SURPRISED BY HOW CALM I WAS.
I DID WANT TO TALK TO MOM, JUST ONE MORE TIME, THOUGH.
WHEN I GOT BACK FROM MY MOM'S FUNERAL, I HAD GAINED FIFTEEN POUNDS BUT LIFE WENT BACK TO NORMAL.
NINE MONTHS LATER, I STAYED HOME FROM WORK AND IN BED FOR WEEKS AT A TIME. I HAD RAIN CLOUDS IN MY HEART. I FINALLY FOUND OUT JUST HOW UNFAIR LIFE COULD BE.
TIME SEEMED LIKE IT WAS MOVING FASTER AND FASTER. SO MANY THINGS WERE DIFFERENT NOW. WE EVEN GOT A NEW HOUSE MANAGER NAMED ALISA AFTER KELLY RETIRED.
VIOLET? I'M WORRIED ABOUT YOU. YOU WON'T COME DOWN EXCEPT FOR MEALTIMES. DO YOU THINK WE COULD TALK?
I WANT TO TALK TO KELLY.
KELLY'S RETIRED. REMEMBER WE TALKED ABOUT THAT?
POOR VIOLET. YOUR WHOLE WORLD HAS CHANGED IN A VERY SHORT AMOUNT OF TIME. YOU KNOW WHAT? I REMEMBER KELLY TELLING ME THAT YOU LOVE PEDICURES, BUT I ONLY HAVE ENOUGH MONEY FOR ONE.
IF YOU DON'T START GOING TO WORK, WE CAN'T GO TOGETHER. HOW DO YOU THINK WE CAN SOLVE THAT?

I DON'T KNOW. I HAVEN'T BEEN TO WORK IN A LONG TIME, AND I'M SO SAD.
WHAT IF, EVERY MORNING THAT YOU GET UP ON TIME, DO YOUR HYGIENE, CHORES, AND GO TO WORK, YOU'LL GET A TICKET? IF YOU CAN GET TWENTY TICKETS, WE CAN GET A PEDICURE TOGETHER.
O-OKAY. CAN I START TODAY?
SURE. BUT YOU'D BETTER HURRY!
ALICIA'S TICKET PLAN DIDN'T FIX EVERYTHING, BUT IT DID GIVE ME SOMETHING TO WORK TOWARDS. AND BEFORE I KNEW IT...
YOU DID A GREAT JOB THIS MONTH, VIOLET. HOW ARE YOU FEELING?
I'M STILL SAD. BUT I FEEL OKAY ABOUT THAT. I'M GOING HOME WITH LUKAS AND EMILY THIS WEEKEND, AND I'M WORRIED THAT THEY WON'T KNOW MY MEAL SCHEDULE OR HAVE THE CUPBOARDS LOCKED.
THAT'S A VALID CONCERN. LET'S GIVE THEM A CALL WHEN WE GET BACK AND TALK TO THEM ABOUT IT. IT'S GOOD THAT YOU ARE THINKING ABOUT THESE THINGS.
AS IT TURNED OUT, LUKAS AND EMILY MADE ME FEEL EVEN BETTER THAN THE PEDICURE DID.
DAD'S GETTING OLD, AND MITCHELL HAS KIDS OF HIS OWN, SO EMILY AND I ARE GOING TO BE YOUR LEGAL GUARDIANS NOW!
THINGS WERE CHANGING, BUT THAT WASN'T A BAD THING. IT JUST MEANT THAT LIFE WAS GOING ON.

A LONG TIME AGO, THE AVERAGE LIFESPAN OF SOMEONE WITH PRADER-WILLI WAS ONLY ABOUT TWENTY YEARS.
THE FIRST EIGHTEEN YEARS OF MY LIFE, I FELT LIKE NO ONE KNEW WHAT TO DO WITH ME. IMAGINE IF THAT WERE ALREADY MOST OF MY LIFE! EVEN IN MODERN TIMES, THERE HAVE BEEN MANY OBSTACLES TO OVERCOME.
BUT LOOK AT ME! I HAVE A HOME, AND A FAMILY HERE AT PWHO. I HAVE THE HAPPY LIFE THAT I'VE ALWAYS WANTED. THE ONE MY PARENTS AND I WORKED SO HARD TO GET FOR ME.
AND YET, I SEE I HAVE ONLY JUST BEGUN. I HAVE HAD THE OPPORTUNITY TO BECOME A PERSON, NOT A SYNDROME.

# How These Books Were Created

The ORP Library of disabilities books is the result of heartfelt collaboration between numerous people: the staff of ORP, including the CEO, executive director, psychologists, clinical coordinators, teachers, and more; the families of children with disabilities served by ORP, including some of the children themselves; and the Round Table Companies (RTC) storytelling team. To create these books, RTC conducted dozens of intensive, intimate interviews over a period of months and performed independent research in order to truthfully and accurately depict the lives of these families. We are grateful to all those who donated their time in support of this message, generously sharing their experience, wisdom, and—most importantly—their stories so that the books will ring true. While each story is fictional and not based on any one family or child, we could not have envisioned the world through their eyes without the access we were so lovingly given. It is our hope that in reading this uniquely personal book, you felt the spirit of everyone who contributed to its creation.

# Acknowledgments

The authors would like to thank the following team members at Prader-Willi Homes of Oconomowoc and ORP who generously lent their time and expertise to this book: assistant director of clinical services Rose Worden, MS, NCC, LPC, CSW; director of clinical services Susan Morris, BSW, CSW; clinical coordinator Lizabeth Moser, MSW, LCSW; director of admissions and consultative services Jackie Mallow, admissions coordinator Melanie Ignatowski, administrative assistant Jayne Gierach, and administrative assistant Rachel Gross. Your passion, experience, and wisdom make this book an invaluable tool for families, therapists, and educators. Thank you for your enthusiastic contributions to this project.

We would also like to extend our heartfelt gratitude to the parents who shared their journeys with us: Joan Black, Dr. Rob Neems, Cynthia Satko Gutkowski, Tymna Lee, David and Janet Johnson, Susan Henoch, and John Jay Coggeshall. The courage, ferocity, and love with which you shepherd your children through their lives is nothing short of heroic.

To the remarkable women who live at Prader-Willi Homes of Oconomowoc and shared their stories with us: Sophie Coggeshall, Lisa Gore, Karen Stege, Tina Soppe, Meredith, and Jenny. Thank you for letting us into your worlds, for inviting us into your times of worry, fear, desperation, determination, love, and hope. You are the reason this book exists.

And to readers of *Ultra-Violet*—the parents committed to helping their children, the educators who teach those children skills needed for greater independence, the therapists who shine a light on what can be a frighteningly mysterious road, the schools and counties that make difficult financial decisions to benefit these children, and finally, those who live with Prader-Willi Syndrome each day: thank you. You inspire us.

# Resources

For further learning and support, the authors of this book recommend the following resources.

## Books, Films, and Curricula

Butler, Merlin G., Phillip D. K. Lee, and Barbara Y. Whitman. *Management of Prader-Willi Syndrome, Third Edition*. New York: Springer Science + Business Media, Inc., 2006. With chapters contributed by 32 experts in the care of individuals with PWS.

Champagne, Marilyn P., RN MSW, and Walker-Hrisch, Leslie, IMEd., FAAIDD. *Circles: Intimacy & Relationships, Level 1*. Available through James Stanfield. Curriculum includes six DVDs, 107 minutes of instruction, one giant wall graph, 50 large laminated graph icons, 50 student personal graphs, 300 peel-and-stick icons, and a teacher's guide.

Davis, Nancy, Ph.D. *Once Upon a Time: Therapeutic Stories that Teach and Heal*. Burke, VA: Nancy Davis, Ph.D. 2006.

*Food, Behavior and Beyond; Practical Management for the Child and Adult with PWS*. DVD. Pittsburgh: Prader-Willi Syndrome Association USA, 2008. Featuring expert speakers Janice Forster, M.D. and Linda Gourash, M.D.

Forster, M.D., Janice. *Best Practice Guidelines for Standard of Care in PWS*. Hubert Soyer, Ph.D., and Norbert Hodebeck Stunteback, 2010. Created by the IPWSO Caregiver Conferences 2008 and 2009. Presentations, abstracts, and guidelines for presenting standards of care in over 80 nations.

Heinemann, Janalee. *Prader-Willi Syndrome Is What I Have Not Who I Am!*. Sarasota: PWSA (USA) publication, Coastal Printing, Inc., 2004.

## Websites and Organizations

Americans With Disabilities Act (ADA), *http://ada.gov.*

"IDEA – Building the Legacy: IDEA 2004," *http://idea.ed.gov.*

International Prader-Willi Syndrome Organisation (IPWSO), *http://www.ipwso.org.*

Prader-Willi Syndrome Association USA (PWSAUSA), *http://pwsausa.org.* To find a local chapter, visit *http://www.pwsausa.org/find-local-chapter.*

Prader-Willi Syndrome Association of Wisconsin, *http://pwsaofwi.org.*

National Organization of Rare Diseases (NORD), *http://rarediseases.org.*

Office of Rare Diseases Research (ORDR), *http://rarediseases.info.nih.gov.*

The Children's Institute of Pittsburgh, *http://www.amazingkids.org.*

## Other Resources

State-specific departments of:

Human or Social Services
Developmental/Intellectual Disabilities
Mental Health
Child Welfare/Children's Services
Family Services

State-specific local education agencies, school districts, and special education cooperatives:

State Boards of Education

# Nathan Lueth

## BIOGRAPHY

**Nathan** came into existence with a pencil in his hand, a feat that continues to confound obstetricians to this day. No one knows for sure when he started drawing or where his love of comics came from, but most experts agree that his professional career began after graduating from the Minneapolis College of Art and Design, as a caricaturist in the Mall of America. Soon he was free-lance illustrating for the likes of Target, General Mills, and Stone Arch Books.

When not drawing comics for other people, Nathan draws his own super awesome fantasy webcomic, *Impure Blood*. He is proud to be a part of Round Table Companies, as he believes that comics should be for everyone, not just nerds (it should be noted that he may be trying to turn the general population into nerds). He currently resides in St. Paul, Minnesota, with two cats, a turtle, and his wife, Nadja, upon whom he performs his nerd conversion experiments.

# Debbie Frisk

## BIOGRAPHY

For forty years, **Debbie Frisk** has worked with children, adults, and families in a variety of settings in the human services field, including acute medical and psychiatric hospitals, long-term care facilities, veteran's hospitals and rehabilitation centers, community-based group home programs, in-home services programs, public schools, juvenile corrections, and intensive residential treatment facilities.

Although she has worked with a wide variety of populations, Debbie's absolute niche is working with children and young adults with developmental and emotional disabilities, severe behavioral disabilities, autism spectrum disorders, dual diagnoses, and complex, co-occurring multiple disabilities. Her particular expertise is in a variety of low incidence syndromes and neurological and genetic disorders, including Prader-Willi Syndrome.

As a consultant for *Insatiable*, Debbie tapped into her education and vast experience to help bring to life the pain and challenges faced by children with Prader-Willi Syndome and their families. She has a dual degree in psychology and social welfare from Carroll College (now University), and a master's degree in social work with a specialization in clinical–physical and mental health from University of Wisconsin-Milwaukee.

After working in all aspects of residential treatment at ORP, Debbie now serves as a vice president for the organization. Utilizing her clinical background and keen understanding of governmental social services systems and special education systems and laws, she helps her clients navigate bureaucratic hurdles to find and receive the most optimal treatment options possible and to secure funding for those services.

Debbie has had the privilege of working with numerous teams of people throughout the years, all of whom have shared the vision, mission, constancy of purpose, and commitment to providing compassionate quality services with a goal of assisting people to achieve their maximum potential and to live as independently as possible.

# Chelsea McCutchin

## BIOGRAPHY

**Chelsea McCutchin** is a wordsmith who believes strongly in everyone's power to listen, act, and change the world. She graduated from The University of Texas at Austin with a degree in English and creative writing, before convincing her native Texan husband and son to come back home to Florida with her. This is Chelsea's second book with ORP, and she is beyond blessed to be the catalyst bringing the remarkable and interesting world of Prader-Willi Syndrome into the greater vernacular.

# James G. Balestrieri

## BIOGRAPHY

**James G. Balestrieri** is currently the CEO of Oconomowoc Residential Programs, Inc. (ORP). He has worked in the human services field for 40 years, holding positions that run the gamut to include assistant maintenance, assistant cook, direct care worker, teacher's aide, summer camp counselor, bookkeeper, business administrator, marketing director, CFO, and CEO. Jim graduated from Marquette University with a B.S. in Business Administration (1977) and a Master's in Business Administration with an emphasis in Marketing (1988). He is also a Certified Public Accountant (Wisconsin—1982). Jim has a passion for creatively addressing the needs of those with impairments by managing the inherent stress among funding, programming, and profitability. He believes that those with a disability enjoy rights and protections that were created by the hard-fought efforts of those who came before them; that the Civil Rights movement is not just for minority groups; and that people with disabilities have a right to find their place in the world and to achieve their maximum potential as individuals. For more information, see *www.orp.com*.

# About ORP

Oconomowoc Residential Programs, Inc. is an employee-owned family of companies whose mission is to make a difference in the lives of people with disabilities. Our dedicated staff of 2,000 employee owners provides quality services and professional care to more than 1,700 children, adolescents, and adults with special needs. ORP provides a continuum of care, including residential therapeutic education, community-based residential services, support services, respite care, treatment programs, and day services. The individuals in our care include people with developmental disabilities, physical disabilities, and intellectual disabilities. **Our guiding principle is passion:** a passion for the people we serve and for the work we do. For a comprehensive look at our programs and people, please visit *www.orp.com*.

ORP offers residential therapeutic education programs and alternative day schools among its array of services. These programs offer developmentally appropriate education and treatment for children, adolescents, and young adults in settings specially attuned to their needs. We provide special programs for students with specific academic and social issues relative to a wide range of disabilities, including autistic disorder, Asperger's disorder, mental retardation, anxiety disorders, depression, bipolar disorder, reactive attachment disorder, attention deficit disorder, Prader-Willi Syndrome, and other disabilities.

**Genesee Lake School** is a nationally recognized provider of comprehensive residential treatment, educational, and vocational services for children, adolescents, and young adults with emotional, mental health, neurological, or developmental disabilities. GLS has specific expertise in Autism Spectrum Disorders, anxiety and mood disorders, and behavioral disorders. We provide an individualized, person-centered, integrated team approach, which emphasizes positive behavioral support, therapeutic relationships, and developmentally appropriate practices. Our goal is to assist each individual to acquire skills to live, learn, and succeed in a community-based, less restrictive environment. GLS is particularly known for its high quality educational services for residential and day school students.

Genesee Lake School / Admissions Director
36100 Genesee Lake Road
Oconomowoc, WI 53066
262-569-5510
*http://www.geneseelakeschool.com*

**T.C. Harris Academy** is a private school option, in the local community, that works not only to stabilize a student's behavior in a therapeutic setting, but also help them thrive academically. Our goal is simple: provide students with the skills they need to function effectively and achieve greater success.

T.C. Harris Academy
3746 Rome Drive
Lafayette, IN 47905
765-448-9989
*http://www.tcharris.com*

**T.C. Harris School** is located in an attractive setting in Lafayette, Indiana. T.C. Harris teaches skills to last a lifetime, through a full therapeutic program as well as day school and other services.

T.C. Harris School / Admissions Director
3700 Rome Drive
Lafayette, IN 47905
765-448-4220
*http://www.tcharris.com*

**Transitions Academy** provides behavioral health and educational services to adolescents in a 24-hour structured residential setting. Treatment services are offered that are best practice and evidence based, targeting social, emotional, behavioral, and mental health impairments. Transitions Academy serves children from throughout the United States.

Transitions Academy / Admissions Director
11075 North Pennsylvania Street
Indianapolis, IN 46280
Toll Free: 1-844-488-0448
*admissions@transitions-academy.com*

**The Richardson School** is a day school in West Allis, Wisconsin that provides an effective, positive alternative education environment serving children from Milwaukee, Beloit, and their surrounding communities.

The Richardson School / Director
6753 West Roger Street
West Allis, WI 53219
414-540-8500
*http://www.richardsonschool.com*

# PRADER-WILLI SYNDROME

## INSATIABLE

A PRADER-WILL STORY

## ULTRA-VIOLET

ONE GIRL'S
PRADER-WILLI STORY

Estimated to occur once in every 15,000 births, Prader-Willi Syndrome is a rare genetic disorder that includes features of cognitive disabilities, problem behaviors, and, most pervasively, chronic hunger that leads to dangerous overeating and its life-threatening consequences. *Insatiable: A Prader-Willi Story* and its companion comic book, *Ultra-Violet: One Girl's Prader-Willi Story*, draw on dozens of intensive interviews to offer insight into the world of those struggling with Prader-Willi Syndrome. Both books tell the fictional story of Violet, a vivacious young girl born with the disorder, and her family, who—with the help of experts—will not give up their quest to give her a healthy and happy life.

# ASPERGER'S DISORDER

## MELTDOWN

### ASPERGER'S DISORDER, CHALLENGING BEHAVIOR, AND A FAMILY'S JOURNEY TOWARD HOPE

## MELTING DOWN

### A COMIC FOR KIDS WITH ASPERGER'S DISORDER AND CHALLENGING BEHAVIOR

*Meltdown* and its companion comic book, *Melting Down*, are both based on the fictional story of Benjamin, a boy diagnosed with Asperger's disorder and additional challenging behavior. From the time Benjamin is a toddler, he and his parents know he is different: he doesn't play with his sister, refuses to make eye contact, and doesn't communicate well with others. And his tantrums are not like normal tantrums; they're meltdowns that will eventually make regular schooling—and day-to-day life—impossible. Both the prose book, intended for parents, educators, and mental health professionals, and the comic for the kids themselves demonstrate that the journey toward hope isn't simple . . . but with the right tools and teammates, it's possible.

# AUTISM SPECTRUM DISORDER

*Mr. Incredible* shares the fictional story of Adam, a boy diagnosed with autistic disorder. On Adam's first birthday, his mother recognizes that something is different about him: he recoils from the touch of his family, preferring to accept physical contact only in the cool water of the family's pool. As Adam grows older, he avoids eye contact, is largely nonverbal, and has very specific ways of getting through the day; when those habits are disrupted, intense meltdowns and self-harmful behavior follow. From seeking a diagnosis to advocating for special education services, from keeping Adam safe to discovering his strengths, his family becomes his biggest champion. The journey to realizing Adam's potential isn't easy, but with hope, love, and the right tools and teammates, they find that Adam truly is *Mr. Incredible*. The companion comic in this series, inspired by social stories, offers an innovative, dynamic way to guide children—and parents, educators, and caregivers—through some of the daily struggles experienced by those with autism.

## MR. INCREDIBLE

A STORY ABOUT AUTISM, OVERCOMING CHALLENGING BEHAVIOR, AND A FAMILY'S FIGHT FOR SPECIAL EDUCATION RIGHTS

## INCREDIBLE ADAM AND A DAY WITH AUTISM

AN ILLUSTRATED STORY INSPIRED BY SOCIAL NARRATIVES

# BULLYING

Nearly one third of all school children face physical, verbal, social, or cyber bullying on a regular basis. Educators and parents search for ways to end bullying, but as that behavior becomes more sophisticated, it's harder to recognize and stop. In *Classroom Heroes*, Jason is a quiet, socially awkward seventh grader who has long suffered bullying in silence. His parents notice him becoming angrier and more withdrawn, but they don't realize the scope of the problem until one bully takes it too far—and one teacher acts on her determination to stop it. Both *Classroom Heroes* and *How to Be a Hero*—along with a supporting coloring book (*Heroes in the Classroom*) and curriculum guide (*Those Who Bully and Those Who Are Bullied*)—recognize that stopping bullying requires a change in mindset: adults and children must create a community that simply does not tolerate bullying. These books provide practical yet very effective strategies to end bullying, one student at a time.

## CLASSROOM HEROES

ONE CHILD'S STRUGGLE
WITH BULLYING AND
A TEACHER'S MISSION TO
CHANGE SCHOOL CULTURE

## HOW TO BE A HERO

A COMIC BOOK
ABOUT BULLYING

# FAMILY SUPPORT

## CHASING HOPE
### YOUR COMPASS FOR A NEW NORMAL
### NAVIGATING THE WORLD OF THE SPECIAL NEEDS CHILD

Schuyler Walker was just four years old when he was diagnosed with autism, bipolar disorder, and ADHD. In 2004, childhood mental illness was rarely talked about or understood. With knowledge and resources scarce, Schuyler's mom, Christine, navigated a lonely maze to determine what treatments, medications, and therapies could benefit her son. In the ten years since his diagnosis, Christine has often wished she had a "how to" guide that would provide the real mom-to-mom information she needed to survive the day and, in the end, help her family navigate the maze with knowledge, humor, grace, and love. Christine may not have had a manual at the beginning of her journey, but she hopes this book will serve as yours.

# REACTIVE ATTACHMENT DISORDER

## AN UNLIKELY TRUST

ALINA'S STORY OF ADOPTION, COMPLEX TRAUMA, HEALING, AND HOPE

## ALINA'S STORY

LEARNING HOW TO TRUST, HEAL, AND HOPE

*An Unlikely Trust: Alina's Story of Adoption, Complex Trauma, Healing, and Hope*, and its companion children's book, *Alina's Story*, share the journey of Alina, a young girl adopted from Russia. After living in an orphanage during her early life, Alina is unequipped to cope with the complexities of the outside world. She has a deep mistrust of others and finds it difficult to talk about her feelings. When she is frightened, overwhelmed, or confused, she lashes out in rages that scare her family. Alina's parents know she needs help and work endlessly to find it for her, eventually discovering a special school that will teach Alina new skills. Slowly, Alina gets better at expressing her feelings and solving problems. For the first time in her life, she realizes she is truly safe and loved . . . and capable of loving in return.

*Also look for books on children and psychotropic medications coming soon!*

CPSIA information can be obtained at www.ICGtesting.com
Printed in the USA
LVOW01s2142031014

406960LV00001BA/1/P

9 781939 418708